Kids On Earth

A Children's Documentary Series Exploring Human Culture & The Natural World

Egypt

By Sensei Paul David

Copyright Information

Kid's On Earth, A Children's Documentary Series Exploring Human Culture & The Natural World: Egypt,

by Sensei Paul David,

Copyright © 2024.

All rights reserved.
978-1-990106-13-2 Kids on Earth: Madagascar Hardcover book
978-1-77957-122-9 Kids on Earth: Madagascar Paperback
978-1-7771913-7-5 Kids on Earth: Madagascar Electronic book

This book is not authorized for free distribution copying.

www.senseipublishing.com

@senseipublishing
#senseipublishing

Get Our FREE Books Now!

kidsonearth.life

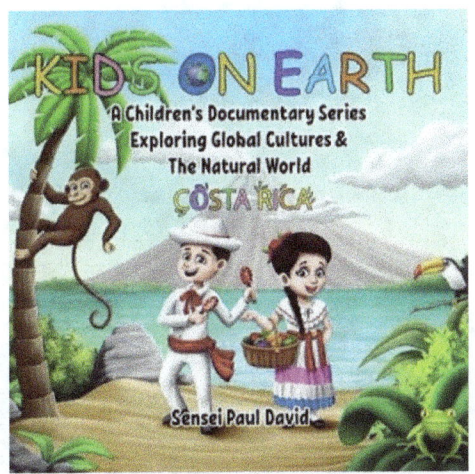

kidsonearth.world

Click Below for Another Book In Each Series

senseipublishing.com/KoE_SERIES

senseipublishing.com/KoE_Wildlife_SERIES

KoE En Español

senseipublishing.com/KoE_SERIES_SPANISH

www.senseipublishing.com

Join Our Publishing Journey!

If you would like to receive FUTURE FREE BOOKS and get to know us better, please click www.senseipublishing.com and join our newsletter by entering your email address in the pop-up box.

Follow/Like/Subscribe: Facebook, Instagram: @kidsonearth

Scan the QR Code with your phone or tablet to follow us on social media:

Like / Subscribe / Follow

Welcome to Egypt!

My name is Farida, and this is my brother Asim.

Asim and I would love to take you on a trip through our beautiful country. It is a very special place, and we cannot wait to share it with you.

Egypt is known as an Ancient Civilization, and this is because Egypt has been around for nearly 5,000 years.

Follow along with Asim and I as we take you on a journey to one of the greatest places in the world and learn about both modern and ancient Egypt.

Are you ready? Let's Go!

FUN FACTS

The name Egypt is from the Greek language, Egypt's name in Ancient Greek was Aegyptos.

The official name of Egypt is the Arab Republic of Egypt and can be found in the northeastern corner of Africa.

The capital of Egypt is Cairo and is home to over 87 million people. That is a lot of neighbors!

Egypt is located near Libya, which shares the border to the west, Sudan, whose border is to the south, and Israel, whose border is to the northeast.

With a grown-up's help, find a map of the world and find where Egypt is located.

FUN FACTS

Egypt is home to the only remaining ancient wonder in the world, the Great Pyramid of Giza.

Like many other countries, the flag of Egypt has gone through a lot of changes throughout history.

The first known flag was from the Rashidun Caliphate, a plain black color, it was then changed to a plain white field when this empire was replaced by the Umayyads in 661 BCE.

It was not until 1915 that Egypt had its first official national flag. This flag belonged to the Ottoman Empire and was red with 3 white crescents and stars.

The flag that currently flies over Egypt features:
- Three Colors – Red, White, and Black
- Gold Eagle

Time to do some research with a grown-up's help!

What other items did the Egyptians invent?

How many of these inventions have you used, or

Have in your home?

FUN FACTS

> The ancient Egyptians were a very clever race. They invented so many different things that are still around today. Some of these things are pens, paper, locks, and keys!

Asim would like to talk to you a little bit more about the land and the special river that flows through Egypt.

The river that flows through Egypt is called the Nile River. The Nile River helps keep Egypt alive. Egypt does not receive much rain, only about 2.5 centimeters or around 1 inch of rain per year.

Each year, the Nile River floods due to the waters that come from its surrounding countries. This helps the farmland that sits along the river to grow crops to help the Egyptians throughout the year.

Do you know how much it rained the last time you had rain?

Look for ways that you can measure how much rain falls when it rains.

Keep a diary and see how much rain you get in 1 week.

How many years of rain would that be in Egypt?

FUN FACTS

Egypt is divided into 2 sections: Upper and Lower Egypt. Upper Egypt is in the South and Lower Egypt is in the North.

90 percent of Egypt is made up of Muslims and identify with the Sunni denomination. Muslims follow the Islam Religion. The other ten percent of Egypt are called Copts, which is one of the oldest branches of the Christian Religion.

Egypt used to be a place with many different deities or gods, and some of these are still looked to today for worship, but not many believe in the old ways anymore.

Do you believe in God or do you have other beliefs?

FUN FACTS

Ancient Egyptians believed in more than 2,000 deities! They had gods for everything, from dangers to chores! Each had different responsibilities and needed to be worshipped so that life could be kept in balance...

Egypt holds a lot of power with its neighbors, and this is because of where it sits in the world, how many people live there, the rich history of Egypt, and its military strength.

Egypt is home to many different valuable resources such as:
- Oil
- Gas
- Textiles or fabrics
- Livestock and
- Chemical Products

All these are then sent around the world and help with Egypt's economy.

Another big part of the economy of Egypt is tourism! We have so many come to visit to see all the treasures that Egypt has and to visit our beaches.

> Faridah what do Economic Goods mean?

> Asim, economic goods are the resources that someone can sell to make money for their country.

Looking at your country, what goods does your country trade with other countries?

FUN FACTS

Some of the places that tourists like to visit are the Ancient Egyptian pyramids. These pyramids were built as tombs for pharaohs and their families. 130 pyramids have been discovered in Egypt so far. The biggest of these can be found in Giza and is called The Pyramid of Khufu.

The healthcare system in Egypt has been gradually increasing and getting better for Egyptians.

During the 20th Century or between 1900- 2000 doctors could be found in a facility that also had schools, social welfare units, and agricultural stations.

The healthcare facilities are often poorly equipped so many end up going to Islamic healthcare centers or traveling to cities to receive health care.

Time to do some research!

With a grown-up's help, using the internet, can find any other fun facts about Egyptian Medicine?

FUN FACTS

The oldest Egyptian medical book are six papyri are called the Kahun Medical Papyrus, the Ramesseum IV and Ramesseum V Papyri, the Edwin Smith Surgical Papyrus, the Ebers Medical Papyrus, and the Heaarst Medical Papyrus.

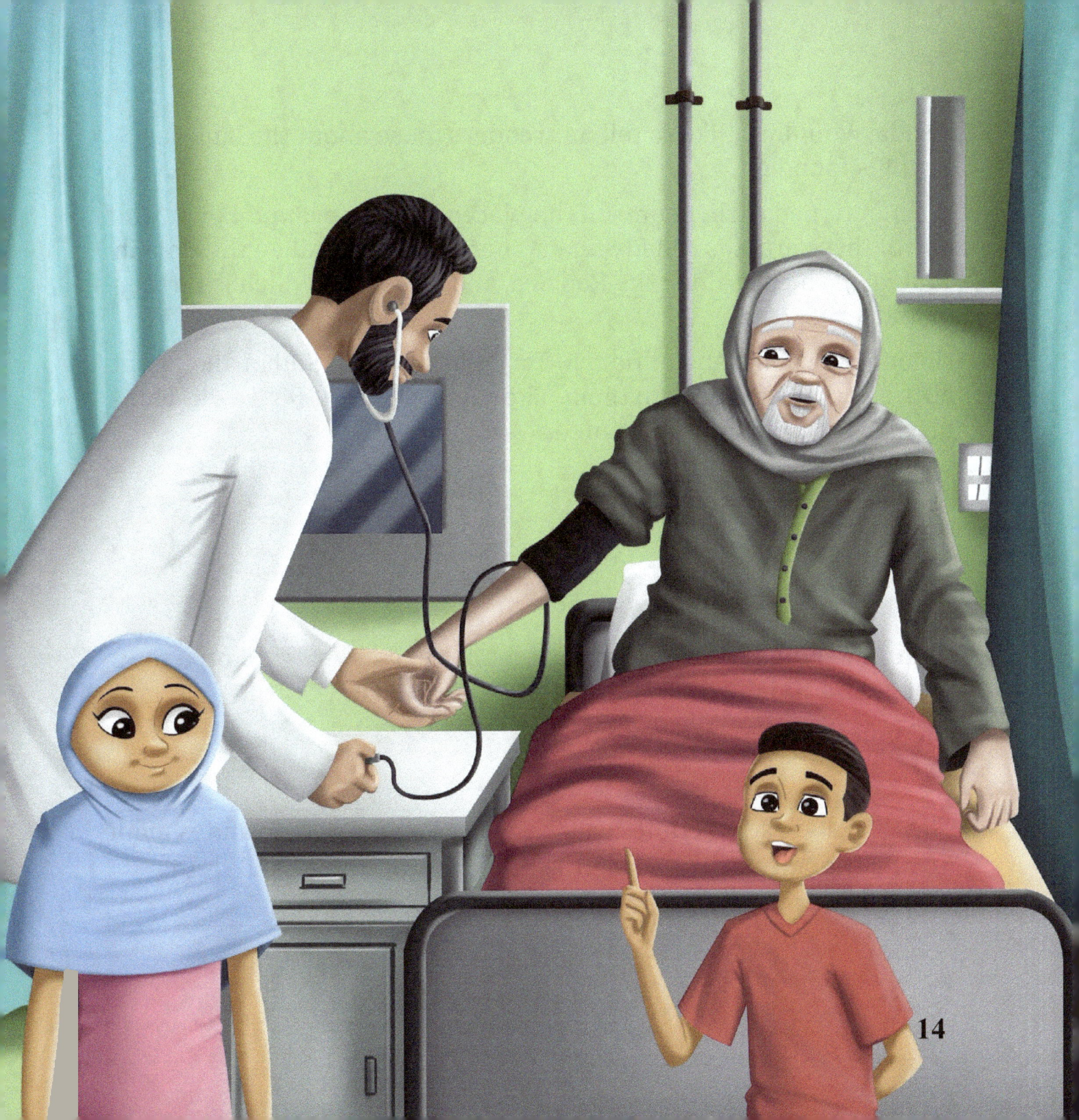

Farida, would you like to tell our readers more about the land that Egypt is found on?

We mentioned earlier some of the places that are around Egypt, and one of these areas is called Sudan. There is a place called the Hala'ib Triangle, which is along the Red Sea, and Bi'r Tawil which is further inland.

No one owns this land of Hala'ib Triangle although Sudan and Egypt both say that it belongs to them. The same is true of Bir Tawil. This piece of land remains unclaimed.

Using the clues in the information above, can you find on a map where the Hala'ib Triangle and Bi'r Tawil are?

Did you find the 2 triangles?

FUN FACTS

The Bir Tawil is sometimes called the Bir Tawil Triangle and is made up of 2 triangles. The 2 triangles share 1 border point and this is called a quadripoint.

Egypt is a really big place and although there is desert there are also mountain ranges. Southern Egypt's landscape contains low mountains and deserts, and Northern Egypt has wide valleys near the Nile, desert to the east and west, and north you can find the triangular Nile River Delta.

It is easy to see on satellite images where the fertile land of Egypt is because of all the farms that are there.

Time to do some research!

Can you find out the following information on the Suez Canal?

- Which Country built the Suez Canal?
- Why was the Suez Canal built?

Although it is known that the current Suez Canal was built during the 1800s, who was the first person to try and connect places through something similar?

HINT You are looking for someone who was a king or queen and was in their country's 12th dynasty.

FUN FACTS

The Suez Canal was built from 1859 to 1869. It officially opened on November 17, 1869

Egypt is broken into four regions, the Nile Valley and Delta, the Eastern Desert, the Sinai Peninsula, and the Western Desert

Half of those that are living in the delta region are peasants or fellahin, with the remaining being landowners or laborers.

The people that live in the valley from Cairo to Aswan are known as Sa'idis.

Those that live in the Eastern Desert are nomadic. Different tribal groups live in this area. These nomads live by herding goats, sheep, or camels. They also trade to get items that they otherwise cannot get.

The Western Desert is home to mainly the Awlad Ali tribe. People in the Western Desert maintain herds of sheep and goats, grow fruit, fish, trade, and make handicrafts.

In the Sinai Peninsula live the Arabs. Many Arabs call the area of Al-Arish home. The next biggest area is Al-Qantarah towards the east near the Suez Canal.

Time to find a map!

On the map can you find the countries mentioned?

FUN FACTS

Cairo is the largest city in Africa and the Middle East. It is also one of the most populated cities in the world.

Egypt is currently run by a Democratic-Republican Government. Egypt has had many different styles of ruling, and this includes a monarchy.

To be the president of a republic, you need to be Egyptian, born of Egyptian parents, and at least 40 years old.

The president is in term for 6 years and may have one more term. The president appoints a prime minister, ministers, and deputy ministers.

The Egyptians had an interesting crown.

What can you find out about the crown that the Pharaohs wore?

With a grown-up's help can you find out the different known Pharaohs that ruled Egypt.

FUN FACTS

The Egyptian Monarchy lasted for 3,000 years with the longest-ruling monarch being Pharaoh Pepi 2. He ruled for 94 years!

The first people to settle in Egypt were hunters and fishermen who settled over 8000 years ago.

Over time they learned how to raise animals and grow crops, trading with different neighbors, and learning to sail boats. In 3000 BC a civilization was born.

How did your country start?

FUN FACTS

Ancient Egypt was often referred to as Kemet. Kemet means black land and it is believed to have come from the soil that was left after the Nile floods receded,

In Egypt, we use the Egyptian pound. The Egyptian pound is divided into 100 piastres or ersh, or 1000 milliemes. The Egyptian pound's symbol is E£ and can also be represented by LE which means Livre Egyptienne which is French for Egyptian Pound.

The Egyptian pound is mainly a paper currency, with notes available in denominations of 200, 100, 50, 20, 10, 5, 1, and 50 and 25 piasters.

What type of money does your country have?

FUN FACTS

The Egyptian Pound notes have several fun features such as:
- The size of the note corresponds to its value. The biggest note belongs to the 200 pound and the smallest belongs to the 25 piaster note.
- Egyptian Pound Banknotes are bilingual. One side is Arabic and has pictures of Islamic Buildings in Egypt, and the other is in English and shows ancient Egyptian motifs.
- The design speaks to the History of Egypt
- All notes have security measures
- The pound has several unofficial nicknames, such as Nekla, ta'rifa, shelen, bariza, and reyal.

Many think that because Egypt lies in a desert area, it would be really hot.

The Climate though is bi-seasonal, or having 2 seasons. Winter lasts from November to March, and Summer from May to September. Winters are cool and mild whilst the summers are hot.

Temperatures in January range from 48 and 65 Fahrenheit or 8 to 11 degrees Celsius. Days last between 8 and 10 hours.

During summer we have 12 hours of sunshine every day, and temperatures can go as high as 106 Fahrenheit or 41 degrees Celsius.

It gets humid in Egypt, and this is evident along the Mediterranean coast which has a high humidity rating.

Rain happens mainly in the winter months, with Alexandria receiving around 7 inches of rain, Cairo about 1 inch of rain, and Aswan only receiving 2.5mm of rain.

The Red Sea coastal plain and the Western Desert are almost without precipitation.

The Sinai Peninsula receives somewhat more precipitation: the northern sector has an annual average of about 5 inches (125 mm).

Time to go hunting!
Can you find the names of the other tropics?
And where they are in the world?
Do you live near one of the tropics?

FUN FACTS

Around the globe, we have 4 tropics. Egypt can be found on the Tropic of Cancer, which divides Egypt into north and south.

There has not always been a stable education system within Egypt, and the schools are usually based on the Qur'an for the primary or grade school and the madrasahs which is Islamic Education.

There are 3 stages of general education:
- Primary – 6 years
- Preparatory – 3 years
- Secondary – 3 years

> Asim, can you tell our readers what the Qur'ran is?

> Of course!
> The Qur'ran is a sacred scripture similar to the Bible.

Have you thought about what you would like to learn as you get older?

FUN FACTS

Egyptian education is fairly cheap. This means that a lot of other countries send their students to Egypt to learn.

The official language of Egypt is Arabic.

Like other countries in Arab, the spoken language is different from the written language.

The written language has not changed much since the 7th Century or between 601 – 700.

Around Egypt, different variations of the Arabic language are spoken. This is due to other countries' influences, such as the English and French. Many Egyptians can speak Arabic, English, and French.

How old is the language where you live?

Is the written word the same as the spoken word?

FUN FACTS

The oldest written language known comes from the Ancient Egyptians and was written 5000 years ago. The Coptic language is the modern form of the Egyptian language.

Faridah, that is a wonderful and cool-looking outfit you are wearing. Can you tell our readers more about our national dress?

Sure Asim!

Egyptians incorporate elements from different groups of people that have played a part in Egypt's history. This includes Ottoman Turks, Europe, Nubian, and other Middle Eastern Countries. We also change the national dress, depending on where in Egypt you are.

Men wear an outfit that has a long shirt or robe which is called a gallibaya. They wear trousers underneath, and then they wear shoes and a turban.

Women wear clothes that are layered and loose-fitting. This is due to both religious beliefs and the climate. Women also wear the gallibaya and a headdress.

A woman's gallibaya is usually bright, although a lot of women prefer an all-black gallibaya.

With a grown-up's help, can you find an ancient Egyptian outfit and a modern Egyptian outfit?

FUN FACTS

In Egypt, there are no religious restrictions on clothing, but they do enforce modesty. To us, modesty is wearing clothing that covers most areas. You cannot wear a bikini or shorts and flip-flops to the shops.

Asim, my stomach is growling. Can you tell the readers about some of the delicious food we eat here in Egypt, while I make us a snack?

Sure Faridah!

There is such a variety of food in Egypt, and these dishes include rice-stuffed vegetables and grape leaves, hummus, falafel, shawarma, kebab, and kofta.

The national dish of Egypt is called Koshari. Koshari is a dish with rice, lentils, chickpeas, and pasta cooked and then tossed with different spices and crunchy fried onions.

Eat Like an Egyptian!

Time to find a grown-up. Together you are going to make an Egyptian feast for your family.

FUN FACTS

Most of the food that modern Egyptians eat today, is what the Ancient Egyptians ate. These are meals that are primarily vegetarian and bread.

Egypt is well known for its pyramids and mummies.

Mummies are usually those that were very important and also from the royal families. They had giant pyramids built and were buried in these giant buildings.

Pyramids are tombs and other than the owners being buried, they also bury some animals and different treasures.

Ancient Egyptians believed that mummification would allow the person's soul to live on in the afterlife.

Can you find all the countries that have used mummification?

FUN FACTS

Egypt was not the only people that created mummies. Mummies have been found in Peru, Australia, and some Pacific Islands.

Looking back on the Fun Facts, we told you that Ancient Egyptians used to believe in more than 2,000 deities or gods. Ancient Egyptians had a good for everything! Each god had a different responsibility and needed to be worshipped to keep life in balance.

The most worshipped gods that are still worshipped today are Ra, Amun, Isis, Osiris, Thoth, Sekhmet, Bastet, and Hathor.

The worship of the various Gods started to decline over time, roughly from 300 BCE to 600 BCE. This was when Christianity became popular, and the churches eventually made it illegal to worship other gods.

Can you find the gods mentioned?

What animal-human hybrid are they?

FUN FACTS

Ancient Egyptian gods are called Chimeras. A Chimera is a combination of animal and human. All of the Egyptian deities had a different animal head that was on a human body.

Egyptian gods

The Egyptian alphabet contained more than 700 hieroglyphs! A hieroglyph is a symbol that represents a letter or phrase of words. These could be pictures of people, animals, and objects.

Hieroglyphics do not have any spaces between the words, and there is no punctuation. To understand what is being written, you have to have some idea about the message that it was meant to say. Hieroglyphs were hard to write, so Ancient Egyptians developed other types of writing that were easier to write.

Hieroglyphs are also hard to read because there is no set way to write them. That means some may read right to left, and other passages may read right to left, top to bottom, or bottom to top. How confusing!

In your country, how did your country develop its writing and reading?

FUN FACTS

Pictures could stand for a whole word called an ideogram, or they could represent a sound which is called a phonogram.

Who does not love music? In Egypt, we listen to a mix of different cultures. Modern Egyptian music blends indigenous traditions with Turkish, Arabic, and Western Elements.

We have Chaabi which is a popular North African Arabic style of music. Chaabi incorporates folk music and blends with pop, rock, or rap.

There is also Egyptian folk music, which includes traditional Sufi zikr and is the closest contemporary music of Ancient Egypt. The music has kept many of the features from Ancient Egypt such as rhythms and instruments.

Can you find any Egyptian Music?

What do you like about it?

FUN FACTS

The harp or the Benet as it was called in Ancient Egypt, is the most popular musical instrument of Egypt. The Bow Harp is amongst the oldest to have survived through time and is characterized by a long, curving neck, and a shovel-shaped sound box.

Time to get some exercise in. Let us stretch those aching muscles. All this reading and I think we need to get up and move about.

Egyptians love sports and you can often find children playing our national sport of Football in the streets of Cairo.

In some parts of the world, the game of football is sometimes called soccer.

Egyptian football has 18 teams that compete throughout the year. Football in Egypt was founded in 1948.

What is your national sport?

FUN FACTS

Have you heard of Gymnastics? Gymnastics was founded in Egypt. Pictures that have been found dating from Ancient Egypt show different Gymnastics dating back 2000 years ago.

Egypt is the oldest tourist attraction in the world. The Ancient Greeks and Romans came to see the pyramids the colossi of Memnon in Thebes. Then the French and British looted Egypt's treasures to fill their museums.

After the British and French visited and took back different treasures from their adventures, more people became aware of Egypt and more and more people came to visit.

We not only have well-known attractions like the pyramids, but also coral reefs, exotic fish, desert dunes, ancient fortresses, monasteries, and prehistoric rock paintings that you can visit when you come to see Egypt.

> Faridah, what is the difference between Geological and Geographical?

> Asim, Geology is the study of the physical structure of the earth, whereas geographically is where you study of places and people.

Where you live, what are your roads made of?

Are there any dirt roads that you travel on?

FUN FACTS

> Egypt sits on 2 continents: Africa and Asia. The Sinai Peninsula which is located in the west belongs to Africa geologically but belongs to Asia geographically.

In the ancient world, there were 7 wonders. Sadly, over time they have been lost all except the one in Egypt.

Have you heard of the Great Pyramid of Giza?

The Pyramid of Giza is located near the capital city, Cairo. Although the Great Pyramid of Giza is an ancient wonder, the biggest pyramid is the Great Pyramid of Khufu, it is also known as the Pyramid of Cheops.

Egypt is also home to 7 UNESCO World Heritage Sites.

These sites are:
- Abu Mena
- Historic Cairo
- Abu Simbel
- Saint Catherine
- Wadi Al-Hitan (Whale Valley)
- Memphis and the Necropolis and
- Ancient Thebes,

Can you find out what the other wonders of the ancient world were?

FUN FACTS

The Pyramid of Giza was built in 2560 BC and took 20 years to build. It stands at 481-foot-tall which is taller than the Statue of Liberty. It took around 30,000 skilled people to build, these included masons, engineers, architects, surveyors, and other craftsmen.

Although Cairo has been Egypt's capital for more than 1,000 years, the government is building a new capital around 45 kilometers or 28 miles away to help ease congestion in Cairo.

The new capital will have the main government departments and ministries, as well as the foreign embassies. This new capital would be known as the New Administrative Capital.

This will help with congestion in the city, and allow more people to live in the capital.

What other countries have had high pollution?

FUN FACTS

Due to the population levels in Cairo, the air quality is up to 100 times worse than what is acceptable around the world. The lack of rain also adds to the situation because the rain cannot clean the air.

If you cannot afford to come to Egypt, then you can find some ancient artifacts in different places around the world.

This is not only in different museums but also as landmarks in different countries. These obelisks stand in London, Paris, and New York City. It is called Cleopatra's Needle. It does not have anything to do with Cleopatra and had been around for over a thousand years by the time Cleopatra took the throne.

Has your country sent any landmarks?

Such as the obelisk to another country?

FUN FACTS

Modern Egyptians have a lot in common with Ancient Egypt. One of these fascinating facts is that ancient Egyptians loved board games. Everyone used to partake in these past times.   The most popular board game that was played was called Senet and Mehen, these games are still played today.

Egypt is full of natural resources. The most valuable minerals in Egypt include:

- Copper
- Tin and
- Gold

It was the Ancient Egyptians who combined copper and tin to make Bronze, making Egypt a military power in the Bronze Age.

Modern Egypt is still known and valued for these minerals, but they are also known for other resources like oil and gas, as well as lead, manganese, and phosphates.

FUN FACTS

All the resources found within Egypt are found in the Eastern Desert and the Sinai Peninsula. This area is known as the Arabian-Nubian Shield.

Weapons from bronze era

56

One of the amazing things that Egypt created was the 12-month calendar. Because of this, if we use the Egyptian Calendar, we are in the year 6264 in the Egyptian Calendar.

The Egyptian months were always 30 days, which was out of alignment with the rest of the world. With all the lost time, the Egyptians then celebrate at the end of the year with a 5-day festival.

What other calendars have been used over time?

FUN FACTS

The most common calendar that is used today is the Gregorian Calendar.

There are only a few festivals held in Egypt during the year. One of the longest festivals is called the Sphinx Festival. The Sphinx Festival is 5 days long and helps bring the ancient to life and to educate people. It is also to help people appreciate the rich and grand heritage of Egypt.

Some of the other festivals that are celebrated throughout the year are:

- Coptic Orthodox Christmas held in January
- Abu Simbel Sun Festival in February
- Sham Ennessim
- Ramadan
- El Hijra

Time to go on a hunt!

Can you find out the name of the festival that is held at the end of the year?

FUN FACTS

Most Egyptian traditions and festivals trace their origin back to the time of pharaohs. The Egyptians also draw many traditions from their religion (Islam).

What have you learned?

Take this fun quiz to see how much you have remembered.

1. What is the National Dress called?
   a. Gallibaya
   b. Capybara
   c. Sombrero
   d. Jambalaya

2. Which of these is not an animal Asim and Faridah mention?
   a. Cobra
   b. Hippopotamus
   c. Locust
   d. Hyena

3. How many continents does Egypt sit on?
   a. 2
   b. 4
   c. 3
   d. 7

4. Which one is the name of the music in Egypt?
    a. Tribal
    b. Jazz
    c. Reggae
    d. Chaabi

5. What is the national food of Egypt?
    a. Crocodile
    b. Koshari
    c. Locusts
    d. Fish

6. Who is the last Pharaoh of Egypt?
    a. Ramses
    b. Ptolemy
    c. Cleopatra
    d. Tutankhamun

7. What can you share with your friends that you have learned from this book?

Answers: 1A 2C 3A 4D 5B 6C

Thank you for reading this book!

If you found this book helpful, I would be grateful if you would **post an honest review on Amazon** so this book can reach other supportive readers like you!

All you need to do is digitally flip to the back and leave your review. Or visit amazon.com/author/senseipauldavid click the correct book cover and click on the blue link next to the yellow stars that say, "customer reviews."

As always...

It's a great day to be alive!

Share Our FREE eBooks Now!

kidsonearth.life

kidsonearth.world

Click Below for Another Book In Each Series

senseipublishing.com/KoE_SERIES   senseipublishing.com/KoE_Wildlife_SERIES

KoE En Español

senseipublishing.com/KoE_SERIES_SPANISH

www.senseipublishing.com

www.senseipublishing.com

@senseipublishing
#senseipublishing

Check out our **recommendations** for other books for adults & kids plus other great resources by visiting
www.senseipublishing.com/resources/

Join Our Publishing Journey!

If you would like to receive FREE BOOKS and special offers, please visit www.senseipublishing.com and join our newsletter by entering your email address in the pop-up box

Get Our FREE Books Today!

Click & Share the Links Below

FREE Kids Books

kidsonearth.world

kidsonearth.life

FREE BONUS!!!

Experience Over 25 FREE Engaging Guided Meditations!

Prized Skills & Practices for Adults & Kids. Help Restore Deep Sleep, Lower Stress, Improve Posture, Navigate Uncertainty & More.

Download the Free Insight Timer App and click the link below:

http://insig.ht/sensei_paul

About Sensei Publishing

Sensei Publishing commits itself to helping people of all ages transform into better versions of themselves by providing high-quality and research-based self-development books with an emphasis on mental health and guided meditations. Sensei Publishing offers well-written e-books, audiobooks, paperbacks, and online courses that simplify complicated but practical topics in line with its mission to inspire people towards positive transformation.

It's a great day to be alive!

About the Author

I create simple & transformative eBooks & Guided Meditations for Adults & Children proven to help navigate uncertainty, solve niche problems & bring families closer together.

I'm a former finance project manager, private pilot, jiu-jitsu instructor, musician & former University of Toronto Fitness Trainer. I prefer a science-based approach to focus on these & other areas in my life to stay humble & hungry to evolve. I hope you enjoy my work and I'd love to hear your feedback.

- It's a great day to be alive!
Sensei Paul David

Scan & Follow/Like/Subscribe: Facebook, Instagram: @kidsonearth

Scan using your phone/iPad camera for Social Media

Visit us at www.senseipublishing.com and sign up for our newsletter to learn more about our exciting books and to experience our FREE Guided Meditations for Kids & Adults.

www.ingramcontent.com/pod-product-compliance
Lightning Source LLC
Chambersburg PA
CBHW080325080526
44585CB00021B/2476